# PAINT BY STICKER

## KIDS

# HALLOWEEN

workman

• NEW YORK •

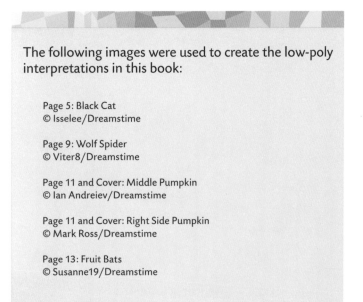

The following images were used to create the low-poly interpretations in this book:

Page 5: Black Cat
© Isselee/Dreamstime

Page 9: Wolf Spider
© Viter8/Dreamstime

Page 11 and Cover: Middle Pumpkin
© Ian Andreiev/Dreamstime

Page 11 and Cover: Right Side Pumpkin
© Mark Ross/Dreamstime

Page 13: Fruit Bats
© Susanne19/Dreamstime

Copyright © 2019 by Workman Publishing Co., Inc., a subsidiary of Hachette Book Group, Inc.

ISBN 978-1-5235-0614-9

Art and design by Claire Torres and Ying Cheng

Workman books are available at special discounts when purchased in bulk for premiums and sales promotions as well as for fundraising or educational use. Special editions or book excerpts can also be created to specification. For details, please contact special.markets@hbgusa.com.

Workman Publishing Co., Inc., a subsidiary of Hachette Book Group, Inc.
1290 Avenue of the Americas
New York, NY 10104

workman.com

Distributed in Europe by Hachette Livre, 58 rue Jean Bleuzen, 92 178 Vanves Cedex, France.
Distributed in the United Kingdom by Hachette Book Group, UK, Carmelite House, 50 Victoria Embankment, London EC4Y 0DZ.

WORKMAN and PAINT BY STICKER are registered trademarks of Workman Publishing Co., Inc., a subsidiary of Hachette Book Group, Inc.

Printed in China on responsibly sourced paper.
First printing June 2019
10 9 8 7 6 5

# HOW TO PAINT BY STICKER®

## 1. PICK YOUR IMAGE.
Do you want to sticker the grinning pumpkins or the glow-in-the-dark skull? It's up to you! Just find the page you want to paint with stickers.

## 2. FIND YOUR STICKERS.
The sticker sheets are in the back of the book. In the top corner of each sheet is an image of a painting page. Find the sticker sheet that goes with the page you want to paint. Both the sticker sheets and the painting pages can be torn out of the book so you don't have to flip back and forth between them.

## 3. MATCH THE NUMBERS.
Each sticker has a number next to it, and each painting page has numbers on it. Match the sticker number with the number on the painting page. Be careful! The stickers aren't removable.

## 4. WATCH YOUR PAINTING COME TO LIFE!
After you've finished your masterpiece, you can frame it, use it as decoration, or give it as a gift.

## ARE YOU READY? LET'S START STICKERING!

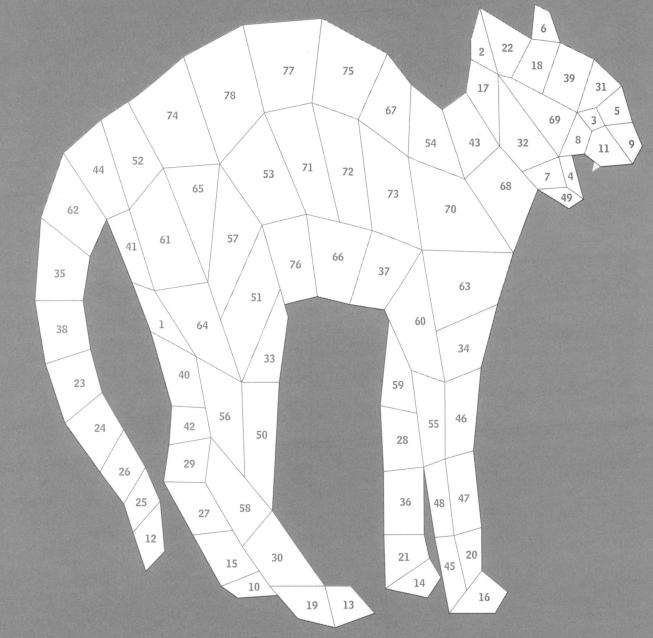

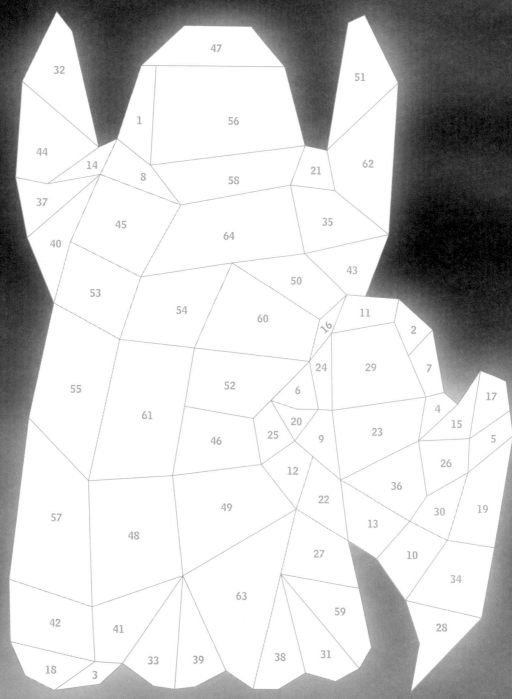

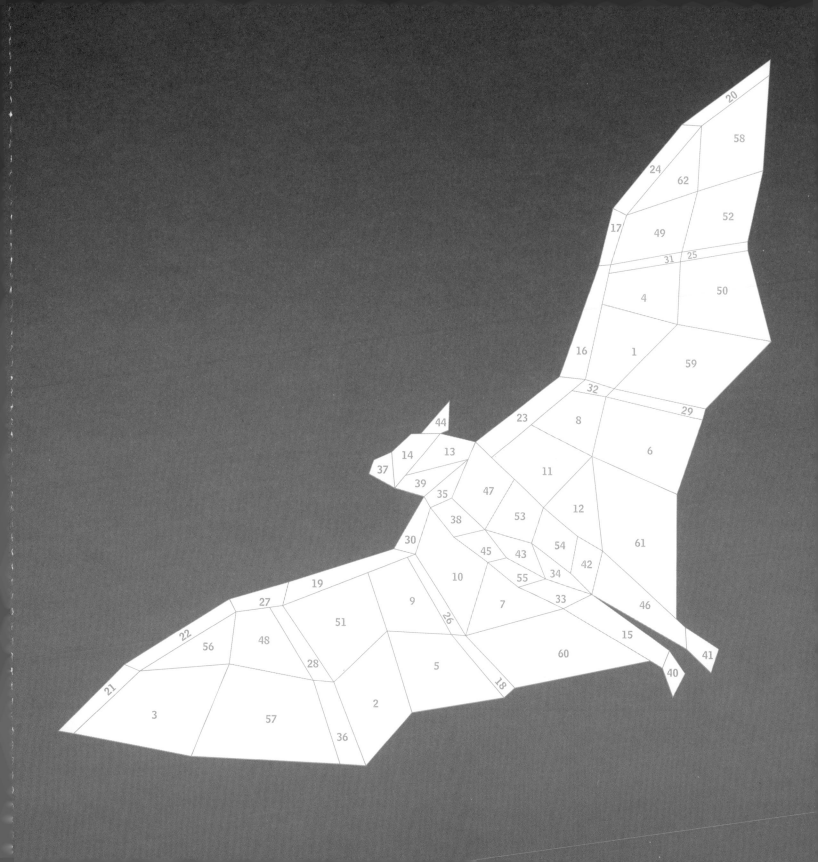

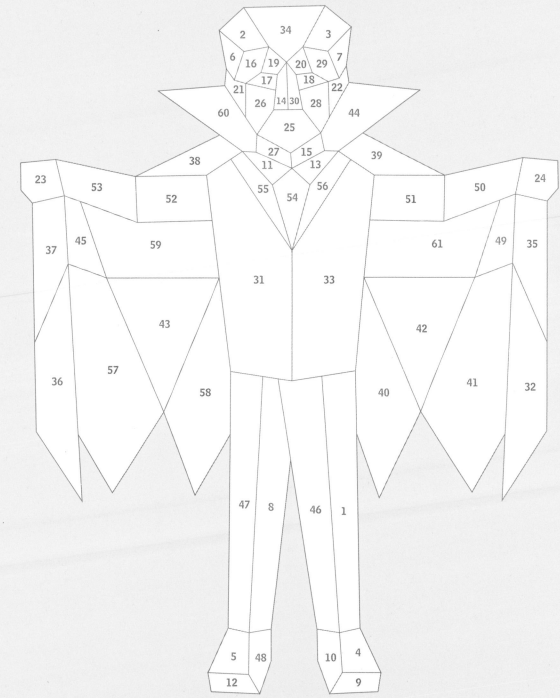

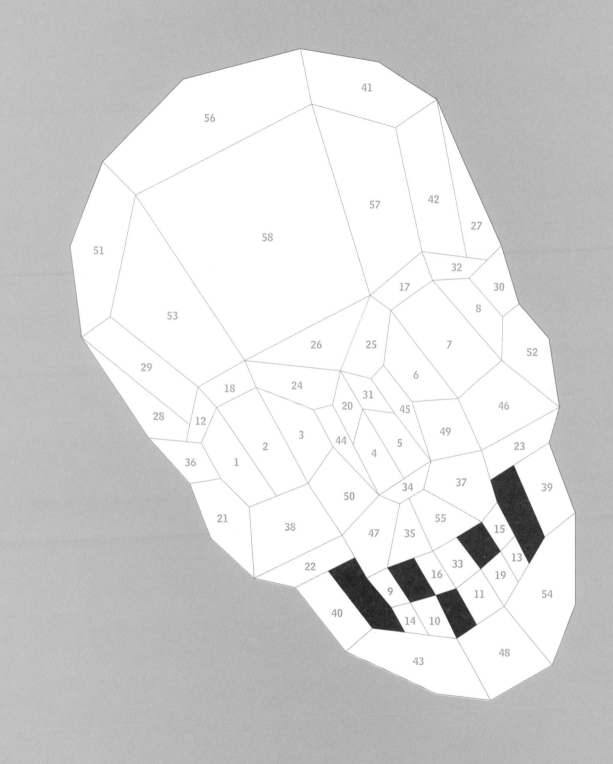

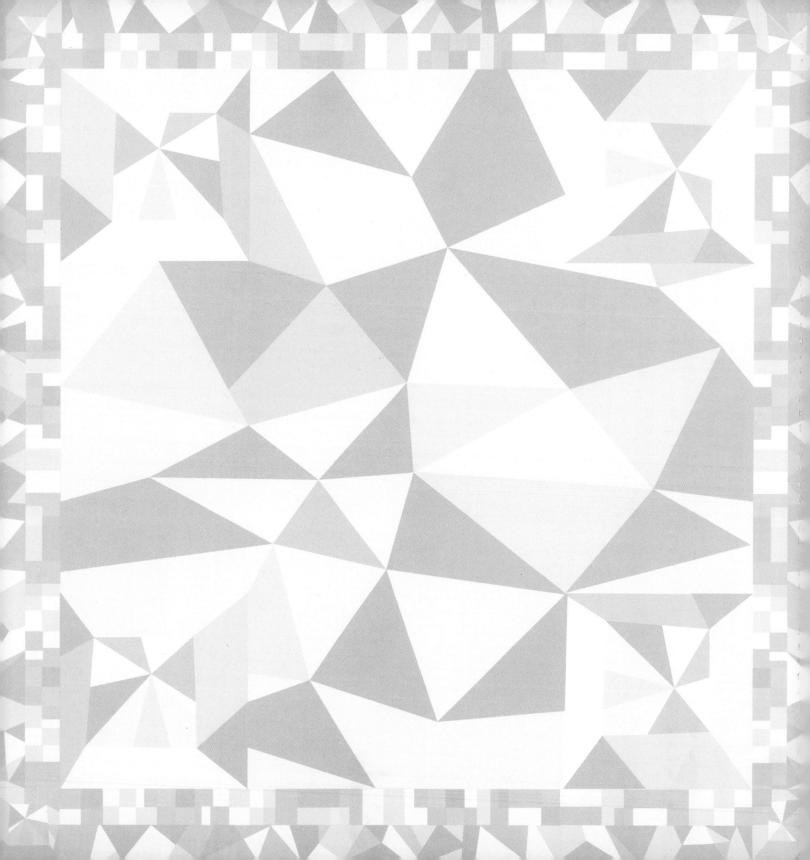

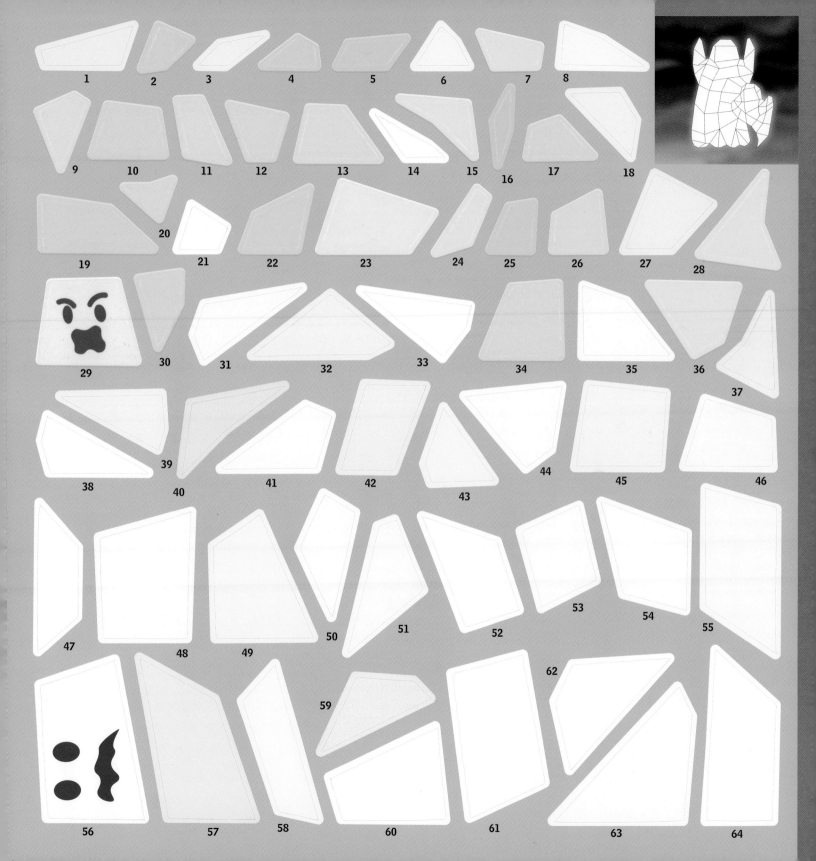

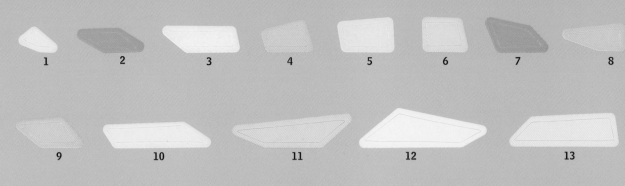

1

2

3

4

5

6

7

8

9

10

11

12

13

14

15

16

17

18

19

20

21

22

23

24

25

26

27

28

29

30

31

32

33

34

35

36

37

38

39

40

41

42

43

44

45

46

47

48

49

50

51

52

53

54

55

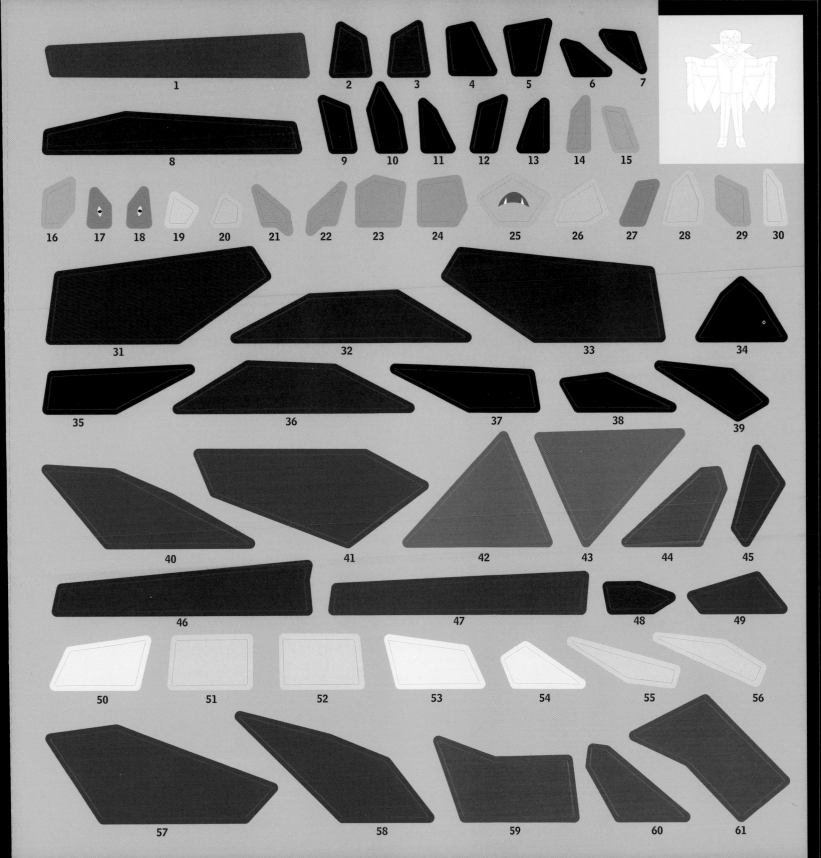

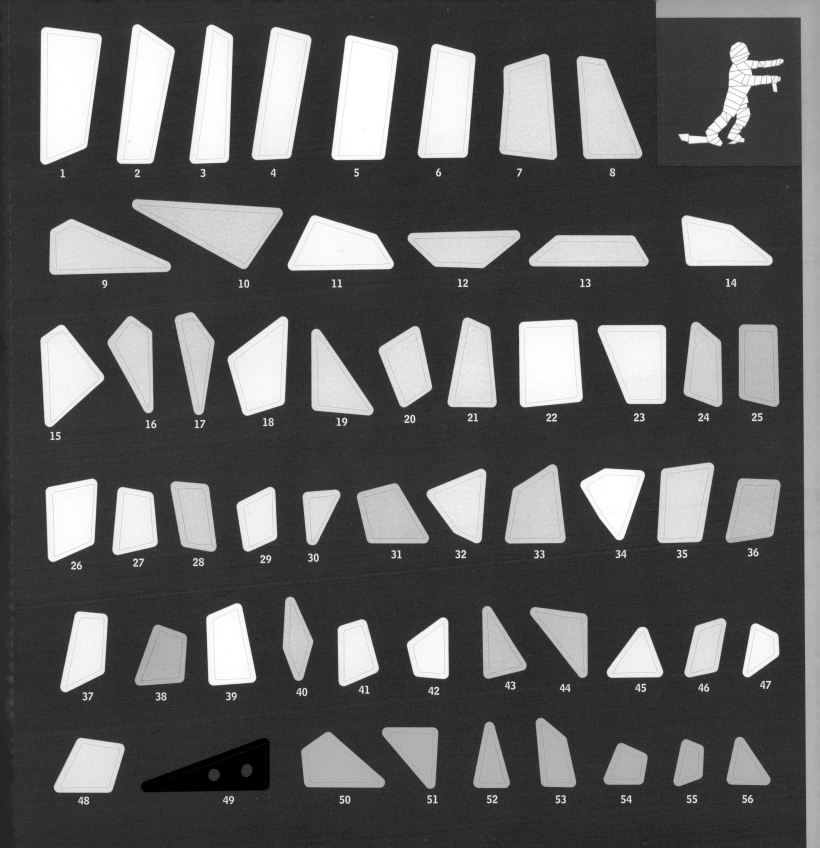